AROUND THE WORLD: Bilingual Weather Wonders
ALREDEDOR DEL MUNDO: Maravillas del Clima Bilingües

Written by Anna Blankenship

Copyright © 2023 Anna Blankenship

All rights reserved. No portion of this book may be reproduced in any form without written permission from the publisher or author, except as permitted by U.S. copyright law.

ISBN: 978-1-963111-00-2 (ebook)
ISBN: 978-1-963111-01-9 (Paperback)
ISBN: 978-1-963111-02-6 (Hardcover)

The illustrations within this book were generated using an Artificial Intelligence (AI) image generator. To the best of my knowledge, these are not copied art and prompts to create these illustrations were of my own creation. The translations within this book are accurate to the best of my knowledge with the aid and support of native speakers.

First Edition

Visit the author's website at www.anna-blankenship.com

This book is typeset in Dekko

To my soon-to-be three bookworms,
you inspire me everyday!

To my husband,
who believes in me no matter what!

To all parents,
continue rocking the hardest job in the world!

-Anna

Seasons

Seasons are different around the world. Weather depends on seasons and where you are in the world.

Estaciones

Las estaciones son diferentes en todo el mundo. El clima depende de las estaciones y del lugar del mundo en el que te encuentres.

Summer
Verano

Fall
Otoño

Winter
Invierno

Spring
Primavera

Summer
Summer days are hot and long. Many people take vacations to the beach and eat <u>ice cream</u>.

Verano
Los días de verano son calurosos y largos. Mucha gente se va de vacaciones a la playa y come <u>helado</u>.

Fall
In fall leaves turn red, yellow and orange, then fall to the ground. It starts to get a bit cold so you might wear a <u>sweater</u>.

Otoño
En otoño las hojas se vuelven rojas, amarillas y naranjas y luego caen al suelo. Empieza a hacer un poco de frío así que podrías usar un <u>suéter</u>.

Winter
Winter is when it gets cold, and it can snow in some places. You can go sledding, throw snowballs and build <u>snowmen</u>.

Invierno
El invierno es cuando hace frío y puede nevar en algunos lugares. Puedes andar en trineo, lanzar bolas de nieve y construir <u>muñecos de nieve</u>.

Spring
In spring, trees and plants wake up. They get new leaves, flowers bloom, and you can see <u>butterflies</u> and bees again.

Primavera
En primavera, los árboles y las plantas se despiertan. Producen hojas nuevas, las flores florecen y puedes ver <u>mariposas</u> y abejas de nuevo.

It is sunny when the big, bright

and warm <u>sun</u> is in the sky. The sun

helps us <u>see</u> and <u>plants</u> grow.

El clima está soleado cuando el gran,

brillante y cálido <u>sol</u> está en el cielo.

El sol nos ayuda a <u>ver</u> y las <u>plantas</u> crecen.

On these days, the sun will <u>hide</u> behind

 <u>clouds</u> a lot. The clouds will <u>move</u> to

let the sun see you sometimes.

En estos días, el sol se <u>esconderá</u> mucho

detrás de las <u>nubes</u>. Las nubes se <u>moverán</u>

para dejar que el sol te vea de vez en cuando.

Cloudy is when soft, <u>fluffy</u> clouds 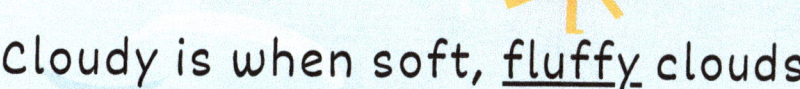 cover the <u>sky</u>. It's like a big, comfy

<u>blanket</u> for the sky.

Nublado es cuando nubes suaves y  <u>esponjosas</u> cubren el <u>cielo</u>. Es como

una <u>manta</u> grande y cómoda para el cielo.

Rain is when water falls from the sky

like tiny drops. It can make the ground

wet, and it's fun to jump in puddles!

La lluvia es cuando el agua cae del cielo

como pequeñas gotas. Puede mojar el suelo

y ¡es divertido saltar en los charcos!

A rainbow is like a colorful bridge in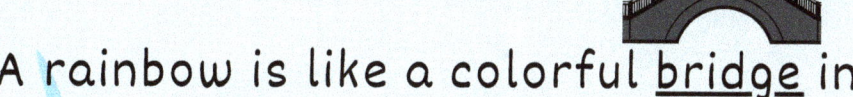

the sky. It has pretty colors when the

sun is out and it rains.

Un arco iris es como un puente

colorido en el cielo. Tiene bonitos

colores cuando sale el sol y llueve.

Snow is soft, white frozen water that   <u>falls</u> from the sky in winter. It's <u>cold</u>  and makes everything look <u>white</u> and soft.

La nieve es agua helada, blanca y suave   que <u>cae</u> del cielo en invierno. Hace <u>frío</u> y hace que todo parezca <u>blanco</u> y suave.

A thunderstorm is when the sky gets dark. We hear loud booms called thunder and see bright flashes called lightning. It's like a big show in the sky.

Una tormenta es cuando el cielo se oscurece.  Escuchamos fuertes estallidos llamados truenos y vemos destellos brillantes llamados relámpagos. Es como un gran espectáculo en el cielo.

Windy is when the air around us starts  to move and play. You can feel it blowing   on your face and making things sway.

Ventoso es cuando el aire que nos rodea comienza a  moverse y jugar. Puedes sentirlo soplando en tu   cara y haciendo que las cosas se balanceen.

Hail is like tiny, icy balls that fall from the sky during a storm. They go "tink, tink" when they hit roofs and cars.

El granizo es como pequeñas bolas heladas que caen del cielo durante una tormenta. Hacen "tink, tink" cuando golpean techos y autos.

Tornado
Tornado

A tornado is a fast, spinning wind like a big tube. They go from a storm in the sky and hit the ground below.

Un tornado es un viento rápido que gira como un gran tubo. Salen de una tormenta en el cielo y golpean al suelo.

Foggy
Neblinoso

Fog is like a soft, white cloud that sits  <u>near</u> the <u>ground</u>. It can make <u>houses</u> hard to see far away.

La neblina es como una nube blanca y suave que se posa <u>cerca</u> del <u>suelo</u>. Puede dificultar la visión de <u>casas</u> desde lejos.

When a sandstorm comes, it looks like   a big <u>wall</u> of clouds. Like if a <u>sandbox</u>  was turned <u>upside down</u>.

Cuando llega una tormenta de arena,  parece un gran <u>muro</u> de nubes. Como si    un <u>arenero</u> se hubiese puesto <u>patas arriba</u>.

Hurricane or Typhoon (depends on where in the world)
Huracán o Tifón (depende en que parte del mundo)

The middle of a hurricane is calm called the "eye." Wind goes in a circle fast around it  and makes waves big and splashy.

El medio de un huracán es calmado, se llama "ojo." El viento gira rápidamente en círculos a su  alrededor y forma olas grandes y salpicantes.

Can you find me in the book?
¿Puedes encontrarme en el libro?

A Note from the Author

To my wonderful readers,

Thank you for purchasing my book! As a new author, reviews mean so much to me and the success of this book series. If you enjoyed "Around the World: Bilingual Weather Wonders," please consider leaving a quick review on Amazon so other parents and readers can hear directly from you. Thank you so much for your time!

Interested in some free activity sheets?
Scan this QR code

www.ingramcontent.com/pod-product-compliance
Lightning Source LLC
Chambersburg PA
CBHW062025050526
44107CB00105B/888